T0193236

FOUR
AFTER
MIDNIGHT

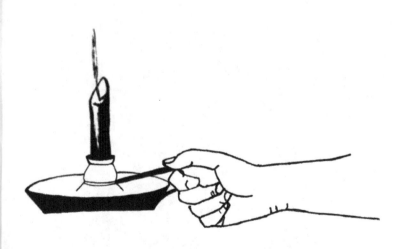

Hezekiah Rory

FOUR
AFTER
MIDNIGHT

Hezekiah Rory

FOUR AFTER MIDNIGHT

iUniverse books may be ordered through booksellers or by contacting:

iUniverse
1663 Liberty Drive
Bloomington, IN 47403
www.iuniverse.com
1-800-Authors (1-800-288-4677)

ISBN: 978-1-5320-8449-2 (sc)
ISBN: 978-1-5320-8450-8 (e)

Print information available on the last page.

iUniverse rev. date: 12/19/2019

Contents

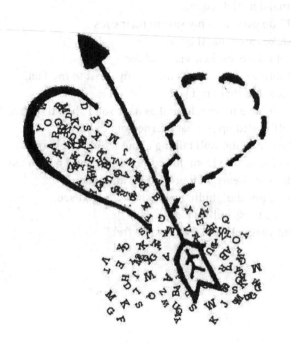

1:00 AM

Mistakes

the good I do they let slide
faster than that lonely kid running home with tears
dripping off his cheeks from his eyes
I can't make it stick on me,
the bad I do overrides my side in their eyes
my mistakes are what they see,
they let it take over their vision of me
they let it live on me like chains on my wrist to my feet,
somewhere out there is a key
I shouldn't have to search for it as a person I should be free
closed off sealed up is what I turned out to be
glass thrown to the wall talking about it didn't help me
I need to break free from this corner of sorrow I put on me
I'm hiding my heart, hiding what I want to be
I'm hiding my soul, hiding what they couldn't see.
Mama stop these bullies please.
I'm eight years old and I want to be free.

There is always that one song that takes you back
to that one time in your life which puts the heaviest
sadness on your chest then it sinks its way through
your skin and into your heart through your veins
and into your head then everything just explodes
till you're boneless on the bed

Dark hoodie

daylight in this dark day
do these thoughts end
can this feeling go away
can these flashbacks fade
I feel dirty to my bones
I can smile, I can laugh
I can continue with my day
no matter what I do
it can't be undone
dark hoodie grey skies
tall trees stupid lies
he hurt me while you walked by
dark hoodie dark eyes
brown skin a bottle of wine
case closed

It's crazy how you can love someone
so much that you let them disfigure
the image you created for yourself.
It's scary because they could just leave.
Leave you looking like that,
and you let it happen

Coffee Stained Tongue

My name was in a letter written by you
now it's burning with clothes I left inside your room,
you can erase me from your memory,
you can't replace me in our memories.
when you grabbed me by surprise,
squeezed me tight & kissed me with your coffee stained tongue,
It made me feel so foolish but lucky all at once.
I tried to shatter everything around me
to keep my heart from shattering,
they said I was going crazy,
but I felt more sane,
more sane than they can
understand.
I was stupid to give you the
attention you wanted from me,
said you didn't get it the way
I gave it all your life.
I caused that crack upon my heart
for letting you use me the way you did,
I was wrong, I played dumb, I was blinded
all because I couldn't get enough of that coffee stained tongue,
I opened my eyes to see what dream you have become and it was
scary one.
I've forgotten about worst nightmares
I could forget about this one too.

She asked

> *Why did you leave me?*

He yelled

> *Why are you so obsessed over our break up!*

As a tear falls down her cheek she says

> *I'm not obsessed*

> *I just seek the answers that I need to put my mind at ease*

> *give me them and I'll leave*

She whispers to herself as his silent mouth walks away

> *I seek the sweet truth my mind craves to give understanding and comfort to my restless and broken body*

Ache

There is an ache in my heart and
half alive butterflies in my stomach,
I flinch when I hear the words *I'm sorry*
what could've happened what could've been
different Is what runs my mind to an unimaginable hell.
Squirming and wheezing with no words
coming out of my head.
My eyes roll to view the window,
I am haunted by the dents in my shed,
there is an ache in every part of me
I am haunted by the thoughts of
scenarios replaying in my head.
I am haunted and I am aching
to the soul of my mortal body
that is traumatizing and I'm sorry
Let the silence of your mouth surrender one day
someday sooner than later.

I tried to be the one
you wanted me to be
but even your desires
weren't enough for you

Do you ever trust that one person that
convinces you that they are there for you
then you open up to them about everything
and it all goes so well but eventually
they get tired of you and you end up
being silent with your feelings
being silent with your problems
and closing yourself off
all because you fear of boring your friends away

I'll always be there for you
- A friend that left

Heavy eyes

My heavy eyes blur out the sunlight
and every hour a weight inside pushes out a stressful sigh
my throat strickens and chest hardens
everyday I wake up then quickly close my eyes,
before that burden in my chest settles for another day,
time is ticking too slow it's like I'm frozen in time,
this dark feeling won't go it's floating like a cell,
digging into my chest making home in my heart,
traveling through my spine my arms and legs
and every vein like it's on a trip polluting me like a plane
It weakened me inside out so let me be
everythings pointless anyways
let me try another day.

Hezekiah Rory

If my tears could break
I bet you'd break them too

We use to leave each other notes on the fridge door and go for long walks along the beach to watch the sunset until the sun was no more. We use to sit by the lake and listen to music and gaze at the stars on the roof until two am. We use to. Until one day the notes stopped, the sun was covered, the music faded and the clouds took over. The rain started and I didn't mind. My tears and I blended in well. No one can tell I was crying my heart out

I only have the footprint
you left on my chest
when you walked
out of my life

Let's reverse time to
the moment that we met
take two turns and
spare each other the mess

Waiting for you

Many moons went through my eyes
while waiting for you I blew up my life
my hours are wasting and I don't even care
my heart is beating to the sound of your lies,
natural lie detector to my bleeding ears they cry
all this chaos and you run into arms that aren't mine,
you blew a kiss I reached out and I missed, you weren't looking
I should've seen the arrow that shot from your lips
my senses are missing I think they're living with you
If only your heart saw what I saw in you,
waiting for you my mind nearly exploded
I could erupt volcanoes and you wouldn't even notice.
Every single day I waited I wrote a line on my skin
until I couldn't recognize myself anymore.
I walked in the rain I tipped over trees
I replanted them I watered them with my tears
my tears you can find on television
next to a tv host on channel four
even to this day I could sneak five cups of coffee to my room,
just to hear you snore two hours before midnight

There is nothing I can't do
that will remind me of you
because I did everything with you

Physically I have wounds and scars
my shadow has none
if I hide everything I am
will I be a shadow too
or just a waste of space

Temporary Mask

The problem with relationships is that we see what we want to see in the beginning and as we go on it's not the behavior that changes, it's them. They're taking off their mask which is why we thought they were who we needed only to find out it is different but you already fell in love. You fell in love with a temporary mask and you can't ask them to change. Once they got you they refuse to let you go. They refuse to put on that mask. They make promises they can't keep. They do things they can't take back and you're left trying a million times to adjust until you're worn out.

I always thought everything I did didn't matter,
until I realized you were blinding yourself,
I always thought my words never meant anything,
until I realized you were ignoring me,
you haven't said a word to me in days,
you haven't said my name in weeks,
which made me realize.
You view me as an evil being.

I screamed save me from my tears
while everybody's ears were on the clock.
but who can hear a body chained down to the past
while everyone is moving fast into the future
including my heart and stable mind,
while I'm chained on these walls,
my soul and body slowly dies,
his story is history someone yelled,
I screamed save me from my tears,
I'm alive just not well

And I Tried

And I tried to be the one you didn't say goodbye to,
to think you're the thought inside my head that takes the focus
off my eyes,
let's just say for a second there I hated your smile,
then you went ahead and closed your eyes in that moment
I was in love with the dimple that formed on the side but I couldn't
let you see.
And I tried very hard to keep you off my mind,
but you ran across at least four thousand times until you ran away.
And I tried to say Goodbye
but instead I cried and said Goodnight with hope
that you'd run back to say it back.
And I tried to be the one but you kept going to find another.

Before you hand me over to pain
tell me you love me one more time

Each of my senses started to numb
as I started to fade in my bed
and even though my dog lied next to me
and the sleep paralysis demon was above me
I could almost hear the screams from my sister
but it was the little voice in my head telling me I'm in danger
I could almost smell and taste the rotting flesh in my dreams
but it was the placebo effect,
fear wasn't present and comfort wasn't near
I was senseless emotionless
I didn't see any lights or fire
it was dark and I was fading
I could hear my mother scream
I gasped so loud and I was breathing
in her arms but was I sleeping

My eyes are no longer the window to my soul,
for now everything is covered in wood,
that explains my brown eyes.
the darkness in my home hides my light
you'd think I'd shine bright now that I have darkness to fight
sometimes I use it to hide.
I'm afraid of knowing the view from the
windows and doors I once knew,
anxiety is glue I'm a hostage in my own home
I don't even try to escape,
Yes, I'd love to go in and out freely but being
inside is comfort for my dim light,
through the crack in the wood I could see a *Crescent moon*,
I can only imagine the freedom of sitting on a ledge so high,
viewing everything else instead of my yard,
to see the waters reflect late at night,
to see the border between the sky and city lights.
Just being free like an owl through the night,
I can only imagine how that must be like.

All the time we took
All the love we made
All the flowers you picked
Just to let it wither away

Even though I know what
happiness is and how to get it
I still play sad songs to cry out
any sort of pain I have left just to
stay in the state of sadness because
I know it will always find me even when I'm happy

Your looks
could kill me
like a cinnamon roll

You're the calm before the storm
then you're the storm
and while I was tricked into a boat going
into the middle of the lake looking for the
seashell I thought needed help
you tipped me over and I drowned for you

You see that I'm upset and I am,
then you ask what's wrong but I don't know
I really don't know what's wrong.
My body is upset for reasons it can only understand
and I don't understand it

                              yet

Our paths crossed so we set
up a tent and table
and had tea and cookies
I wonder how long will we last
before we get bored

One Breath

I was just a boy who saw the signs,
a silent tongue with mouths swarming my mind,
trust issues were mine only because I was alone
for all my life until this day,
thinking I found a forever at sixteen, how naive,
with one breath he told me he loved him,
with another he told me he missed me,
months have gone by with the repeat of the
same silly words that got me,
I thought that each I love you each I miss you was an
arrow of love shot into my heart with each letter I knew when
the time came something would trigger,
I told myself off hoping you were the one to put down that gun.
One day with one breath you said "we're done"
with one grasp followed by a squint,
you ended mine
I should've listened to myself

I am the city lights you thought were so beautiful
and when the black out came you were lost.

Until you saw a glowing silhouette and chased it to
the outskirts of my small town.

I lost you when I found my light

Would you kiss my lips
if they were blades
and you couldn't resist

Alien

All of this mess makes me want to tidy
but my mind is too tangled
it'll take hours to unbind me but
by then I'll already be asleep
all of this space and I still juggle in the corner,
falling on the ground my fires burning out,
No, I'm not an alien I'm a human safe
I hide myself, I tape my mouth
I sit inside all day dreaming about my lighter days
No, I'm not an alien I'm a spirit that was seen.
blown in by the wind staying off the grid
No, I'm not an alien I'm just tangled in anxiety.

You're a Puzzle
that I'm blind to

They say I'm allowed to feel these feelings
but like lighting up a match and blowing it out
my feelings fill the room and their empathetic
ability absorbs it and just as much as I feel they feel
then it gets messy and I shut down.

Error

You think I'm upset about stupid little things but
It's not about that. It's about the pattern in which you've been
treating me lately and that's what gets to me.

Think about it

Seasons Stones

A stone can grow without us noticing.
so can pain. well, at least this pain
when the season transitions,
It changes shape but that's all.
The pain is still the same.
I know this because I can feel it in my bones,
my bones become so weak that milk doesn't do a thing.
I thought of myself as a leaf that fell from the family tree.
and that the leaves that fell before me would catch my falling heart,
but that pain resided in them too
they could barely hold the petiole they carry
they couldn't glue their shreddings back on
and four times a year
I'm the same as our crumbling leaves
and never the same in society.
thanks to the shape shifting pain I will never recognize.
pain I will never be face to face with
pain I call seasons stones
pain I keep in the pockets of my bones
I am doomed to my bed for a season

Hezekiah Rory

Your apology had a lot of scratches and breaks,
It wasn't pure enough to bandage the wounds you opened,
I looked in the mirror and saw pain all over my face,
I told myself *I Love You* until I was screaming at the mirror,
the mask you gave me instead of helping me find myself stuck on.
I listened to your voice and heard a poorly produced song.
The angels weren't dancing and my nerves were rattling.

It's hard to rewrite what you burned

Toxic Mouth

I felt like a flower you loved and kept around for the beauty and comfort.
Overnight I withered and you started raising your voice in the most frightening tones because you thought you didn't bring me happiness. You do.
I looked down in the sunlight that is supposed to make me rise.
I wish you watered me daily so I could at least cry something other than the dirt
my face fell into. My neck is sore and its hell on my body I can't lift and unbind because you hold my withering body in this position with your toxic mouth

I figure if we plan ahead
you'll want to stay and
achieve what we said

I don't know if you ever think of me
because I think of you almost every second
of every day and it aches my mind
I just want it to stop

You yell until my hair turns white from fear,
you swing and swing until I scream,
permanent marker can't erase with an eraser
the way you fell onto your knees like you were in a movie.
I couldn't help but feel like I was stuck in a bear trap
struggling and hugging the bear that claws my skin
until the scratches on my bones are revealed
your hugs of healing are hugs of discomfort
and I want to escape but the love I have for you
wants me to let you believe you are healing me
and I hope you believe

how many teardrops could follow the same
wet trail down my cheek before one breaks off
how many life times can I live through the
same pain you put me through
If only I could remember my past lives
If only I could count each tear that broke
and then maybe I wouldn't hurt myself so much

I framed your words in my
heartless club so party goers
with no senses can laugh at
what you said to me

I feel unsafe in places I once
found comfort in and I found
comfort in the most dangerous
places I don't belong in

Let us pray to let us love,
maybe us meeting was bad timing,
two turns down the same road
taking turns holding our crescent candles,
chasing down the angel of destiny,
to change our ways,
to change our paths,
so we can meet again before it's too late

Old Candle

There is nails in my bones,
I'm leaking through my wounds,
I'm crawling and breaking fingers
to make it through the day.
screaming your name
but like a cat you stare at me and run away.
hold me in your arms
my blood is becoming
a red rug on your floor
can you hear me
I'm trying to break through my skin
with all these holes and removal of bones
It only gets tighter
don't you see that I'm suffocating
I can't live in this body anymore
I'm reaching for an old candle
toss it on me give me that flame
burn this flesh to ash
release me from this pain

I gave you so many kisses
while you played your games
too bad you weren't the video
game type of guy

The day I buried my words for you
something evil sprouted out of the ground but it's okay.
They weren't mine to kill

The glass ain't so pure when it's painted
be honest when you reassure
I know you really love me
the most truest
love you could ever give
do I deserve it
aren't I just an idiot
I make scenarios in my mind
I sometimes follow through
I make mistakes
mostly out of fear
I wish I could trust me
the way you trusted me
I wish I didn't break it
dropped it and cracked it.
The glass ain't so pure when it's in pieces

Nothing but a rainy day can erase the mark you left on me,
If only it were that simple to erase the dent your hand left on me,
I'd run in the rain until I get sick just to see if it would do anything
nothing but a sunshiny hot day can burn the skin you touched
all these handprints revealed themselves
some places I never knew you touched

When it comes to you I don't know what's the truth
It's a gamble when you open your mouth

Abandoned Home

The day our family split apart and everyone ran
in different directions I stayed home.

Week one - I was taken to my another families home because I was too young to stay alone

Week two - I took my friends to our home. We snuck through the window and I sat on our couch and I cried at the sight of our broken home

Week three - I took some belongings with me to my new home. I wanted keepsakes to remember our happy family days

Week four - I went back alone. I saw a homemade present of mine become trash on the floor. I held onto it tight and cried.

Week five - I saw renovations were done. I could still enter our home so they weren't very tight on security.

Week six - our home was thrown across the yard. Our doors and dressers. Our height measurements on the door frame and gifts. Broken.

Week seven - the door was locked and I cried trying to open it. I tried the windows and they were broken but I couldn't fit in. I sat outside to remember our yard. The days we played baseball or dug holes in the ground. Even the time we just sat on the grass and be silly together.

Week eight - A new family moved in. I couldn't enter anymore. Even with the door wide open it wasn't open for me.

When no one fought for our home that's when
I knew we'd never be the same again

Every time my Lips
call for a kiss
you hang up

You think you know all of me when you don't know that I know what it feels like to die. You don't know I know how it feels like to not breathe and want to scratch myself until my bones are showing. You don't know I know how it feels like to want to drown myself in alcohol until I'm sparkly clean inside. You don't know how I'm so chained on my pain and reaching for a solution brings more scars and torn skin than staying where I am. Maybe that's why I'm sitting on a seat of anxiety and eating a pill of depression each day because it's an uncomfortable comfortable place that I know so well

Do you really want to have a first date
a first kiss
Do you really want to watch our movies and
listen to our songs
Do you really want to start another journey
our journey
Do you really want to go through all that again
with someone new

I was in love with you while you were hurting,
pounding every brick wall until you opened up
your knuckle. I would listen to you while you'd
talk about things you needed to get out,
things that would sometimes hurt me.
I was waiting for you every time you told
me to go away and never come back.
I was there for you when you needed me and
I stayed through all the fireballs that hit me
every five seconds and even with fifteen warning
signs slapping me in the face.
I thought I was being strong but I shouldn't
have mixed that six letter word with another

Hezekiah Rory

How do I get over you when the streets
got your name written down the lines like
every signature you signed flew off the paper.
How do I forget we ever existed when a whole
part of our history is us living
How do I forget our moments when they're
playing on every channel on television
How do I forget you like you forgot me.
How do you do it so well

You could make
a candle flame cold

The surface was clean and had the best smiles
while we were stabbing ourselves in the back
lying to every face that looked our way.
Behind the curtain we created hell only
to each other for each other
lust was our chains and the worst part is
that you can never escape hell.
Screaming, Tired, Fires
gasoline isn't working now.
If only our light was eternal then maybe
we wouldn't be so distant.
Special occasions down the drain
arguments in front of our parents
storming through our favorite moments
lightning strikes, fire lights
scrying through the skies
just to find peace of mind
our home was burnt way before the fire.
The inside was charcoal and rotting flesh
was sweeping through the vents

Never destroy what you
love because it could
destroy you right back

My mind won't let the words leave my mouth
knowing it could blow up years of my life
I overthink about you overthinking
you shake your head no when your mouth says yes
I'm in my head I'm in my mind I'd rather get out
organizing words organizing feelings
just to be comfortable in my skin
I'm overthinking and you're okay
I wish I could read you like a book
and maybe I'd know what's the truth
my heavy feelings sink into my stomach
making me sick knowing the truth
is the medicine I can't get

The dust I collect from
not having any returned
affection is blinding me
from the heart I once knew.

I think I'll miss you the most
when you're squeezing someone else's thighs
thoughts of you with someone new is popping my ears
It flies me through the air only to crash and burn.
All the potions I'd take to forget I'm happy for you.
the leftover honey you left on my lips from when you
kissed me goodbye turns acidic and opens my scars.
A secret you kept from the one you say is meant for
your arms like a key she fit into your shoes and oversized sweaters.
A model I can't compete with.

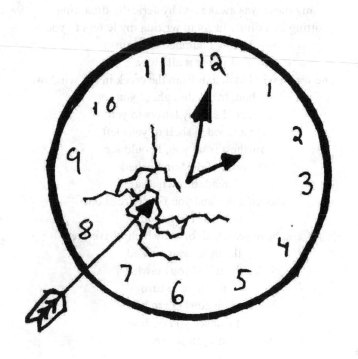

2:00 AM

Letters to you

Nights were tough and lonely
one two three four am
my muse was awake and hysterically dreaming
sitting in a dimly lit room writing my letters to you
Is how I numbed the pain
I wrote it all away.
The warm wind blown in from the crack in the window,
bought the thought of you.
I could see my letters to you
On a wooden shelf to your left
furthest from you, I could see
piles of dust untouched
unread, thrown away,
shoved aside and you finally read one
that was my goodbye.
You have searched for me which I have seen
the miles you walked
the miles you crawled
nowhere to turn
I'm nowhere to be
I can see you darling
do you see me?

beautiful place painful memories
that's what it is, that's where I am.
my roots are cold but it's my home

tears fill my eyes till they shine
then they sink back in
a sweet river I need to feel
less stones and concrete
a release I need to become full,
and not crescent
soon I'll get what's coming to me.
returning to my empty leather
of a triggering letter
I will swarm this body
with all lifes pleasures

I want to be the part of
the story you read
over and over
just to feel happy again

We're like land mines
each and every one of us
one day you'll explode and I'll explode
that's not in a literal sense obviously
what I mean is we will give a pain
and hearts will be broken.
there will be empty cavities in their chests
even if you think you don't mean anything to anyone
they'll bring their closest moment of you and them to the surface
and hold it close with clenched wrists
until they decide they are ready to slide
it into the back of their mind
and there you are,
in the back of the mind
you'll come to the surface sometimes
only sometimes
that's the truth
and it isn't terrible

I feel like I've been asking for too much
but realized you started giving me so little of
what you use to give me so much of

I can try to run from feeling second best unwanted
and not important but what is there to run from if
nothing is chasing me

They got me

Clouds

Memories repeat in my head over and over
like the thought bubble is still there
sometimes they flow right passed,
sometimes they bring dark clouds to play,
trauma stings like lightning hitting the brain,
fear sneaks up on me like a tornado in my veins,
my mouths so dry it whispers tsunami,
when the clouds swirl and disappear
my flashbacks do the same,
when dark clouds come a lot of bad happens and I'm afraid.
when clear skies come I wonder what will happen

You've ruined some pretty
good music with the memories
you left me

Don't

Sentences you said are on repeat like a broken radio,
the lies I was eating and believing
I think I'd be better off breathing in carbon dioxide
please, don't talk about how we use to be,
don't show me any love you still have for me,
I remember it all too clearly I'm trying to wipe it from my memory.
so many words so many promises just to crack in half,
I couldn't help but absorb the truth coming from your actions,
retelling our story didn't put me under, my ears weren't having it,
the chaos in my head wasn't having it
I remember it all too clearly I've had nightmares waking me,
I find comfort in the empty side of my bed knowing you're not there.
your troubling hands no longer scrape my thighs,
and while you're chasing your head down the hill
I'll be collecting my senses and growing a garden on my road,
to blind you by planting beauty
something you've never seen
something you always throw away

You shattered my heart and as I was picking up
the pieces you kicked them all away
I stared up just to see you glare and growl in anger
it took me months to find every piece except one
the dullest one but it completed me
the part of you, you left on me I hope stuck to your shoe
it was like an itch I couldn't scratch, a frustration to my skin
there's an emptiness, a hole on my body
it was my job to heal it and you bet I'll fill it better than you ever did

You have showed me
the understanding of sad songs
I've had on repeat for years

Grey

Our flame pinched into smoke and that's when our world turned grey.
We were once flying colors now we're the raging sound of television static,
we're strangers that met now we're strangers that left,
everything went colorless when we stopped drawing in the lines
we left our pens and markers behind no more scribbles no more sky,
just sketching tools with no hand to hold
just a white sheet of paper we ripped up threw in the pit and covered it in fuel.
Our poetry is in ashes picked up by the wind now floating through the trees
the smoke we inhaled slowly kills us but that's pain in a lethal form we expected but never knew.
Our love is grey and faded like our flame
and there flew away our blank paper planes

You bought me a necklace
then you said a sentence
now I wear your words around my neck.

You get cold
laying there not realizing what is happening
from your feet to your knees an unfamiliar breeze
or so you think
your knees to your waist to your chest
it gets colder and starts to burn
out of control tears, scribbled fear
what's going to happen next?
shaking from your head to toe
cold feeling please go
frozen in time
time please let me go
one last gasp and darkness takes control
beep, beep, beep,
blurry vision, bright light
squinting my eyes tight
I've survived
and now I *Ache*
in every part of me
I hope this fear fades

Like driving down a highway,
I saw the signs but kept going anyway

Perspective

In the beginning you had a choice to pick up or to not
to hold a heart you must be careful.
As your hand silently swept through the air
you picked up and held that delicate piece with tight wrists.
Nail beds surrounded you as you walked away from that altar
tiptoe not for the silence but for the crows loudly cawing
at the sweet sugary heart you hold in your hands,
driven to insanity your mind needs a remedy,
bleeding feet from dropped glass digging deep into open wounds
tears and blood mixed so fast under toes and onto land.
blood puddles left a trail now you're on the map.
You don't know that their screeches and caws are my heart beat,
my heavy stone cold heart dances from the crows not your hands.
Don't drop it

They say you have to love yourself before
loving anyone else but in some messed up
way I started loving myself by loving you
in the back of my mind I knew
I gave you the opportunity to break me.
That was a risk I took only for you

Hiding from Love

I know you're somewhere in our dark land,
I know you're hiding in the shadows and fog shooting every heart
arrow,
I feel you touching my silhouette every chance you get
I feel your eyes on me like sun rays hitting my skin digging into me
I feel your presence showering me in warmth and serenity
I hear your footsteps in the rustling of leaves
and the click click of branches breaking,
I can see your sparkling prints in the soft land,
You're so unknown to me even though you're standing right in
front of me
Just be a stranger to me I'm afraid of you picking on me

Love Seeking Me

You're masking every traumatic moment with me,
stop running from love and dodging every spark I give you
help me help you see me,
don't be afraid to let me find you,
don't let this dark world define love for you,
I will find you and I will show you how to find me.
One day you'll see the beauty that love is
and the beauty of how it is independent
within you

I say I forgive you when I don't feel it down inside
I say it so you can be at ease with yourself but you and I
know that I don't mean it until I truly say it in that certain tone
the presence of each other is uneasy like the itching of freshly cut
hair in the fabrics of our clothes
the only thing holding us together is the distance and silence strings
that someday I will call you and tell you I forgive you in my tone
we see each other and the uncomfortable itch peeks itself onto
our skins
the vibe I bring lights like a match and fills the air
all we do is stare and hide behind our hooded sweaters
trapped in a room by hope that one of us will say something but
our mouths are taped with the problem clearly written in the air

When you left the moon appeared
because you didn't think I deserved
the light from the sun so you took it with you.
don't worry I'm a selenophile
not a sunflower

I try to speak the madness in my mind
I end up walking into traps noticing after
they had my name written on the side,
I take myself to the padlock that can only
unlock by the shape of my body,
chaos erupts in me and flower pedals
explode out of my mind,
I speak the truth, threats are made and
I'm running to the door tired of turning
to stone when I stare into those eyes

The return of you has got me on my knees
I stood up because you're no longer a sanctuary

I've seen so much messed up
reality that messed up fiction
doesn't phase me anymore

Everyone will like those nice things you say about yourself but the moment you say something negative people don't pay attention in hopes someone will deal with you and get you on your feet again so they can praise your recovery.

Even though we are together,
In the dark cold night I screamed
Even though we can't be without each other,
I ran away by myself to weep,
Roots can split in two,
So can bones and trees too,
Roots can wrap each other,
So do my earphones,
We unraveled and split but
sound still comes to my ear,
honey, it's just for a short while
till we're back in the pocket of our home.

when you said *you better not write about me*
you should have known my next move would be
a pen and paper

Secret Keeper

Remember when you told me
baby, Please don't worry.
I tried to hold my hand out wide
I let go and your hand fell into mine
I can feel something underneath your skin
fighting like a feeling that you're holding in
I can feel the tangles and twists of your veins
the scratches and dents on your bones, deep down.
Keeping yours but always spreading mine
I trusted you and you whispered to your favorite people
open mouth when it comes to throwing me down.
Little Lying Secret Keeper how can you,
you must feel a little guilty
Let's say I asked a simple question would you get angry?
Would you?
Little Lying Secret Keeper how did I get this treasure
to make me feel insecure,
hiding all your favorite people,
lying to my face with your little guilty face
I don't understand why you tell me you'll tell me anything I ask
then I hide behind the couch
while you're throwing things around.
screaming at my loneliness
to scare it back into me
when it tries to escape.
I don't know why you
think that you make me happy
when you hide all these people around me
I don't know why.
Do you?

Let me be a mirror for your words
then let's hear you call me toxic

I don't want to fight anymore,
about the same old reasons that hold me to the door
I don't want to scream anymore
forces that tie my fingers to the floor
I don't want to lose my voice anymore
speaking through my hands and notepads,
I don't want to sleep on nail beds and go through doors
that aren't meant for me.
I don't want to be a prisoner of your love anymore.
I won't do it to myself

The trees outside release the leaves they grew
if only it were that easy to erase our history strings
a razor can trim those little snakes but some
insects always grow back. Your scent is infinite
and my remedies aren't permanent.

I'll whisper in your ear maybe I'll appear,
can you hear me darling do you see me.
I'm whispering and the moon is crying
wake up the world is ending.

Silly little antique shop with keys jingling from being dropped.
with a weird text written on the side followed by sixteen hundred
be careful human, It can open anything.
While you were sleeping I was going to whisper in your ear
hoping to appear in your dream.
Until I saw a weird shaped indent on your skin,
silly thinking, I put the key in and like a shoe it fit
you really know how to make things surface deep,
I saw the minutes made of lies, anagrams and
notepads. Hours of fake plants rotting through our life
It was my time to know now I'm out the door.
Sweeping my feet across the pavement dancing in a baggie
sweater that was yours now it's mine

Not Ready

You ran to me while I walked away slowly
grabbing my arm and kissing my lips.
I wasn't ready.
It's only been a second and I'm stunned.
I'm also short and standing next to you was
like standing next to a skyscraper.
The height difference that people covet.
I looked up to you I slowly smiled
and gave into my feelings as you leaned in
I feared you'd fall me on me and crush me
to be honest you did way more than that.
My biggest mistake made seconds
before trouble dissolved in my mouth.
You walked away and said *I Love You*
I guess it dissolved in yours first.
the *I love you* pill that makes us go crazy if
we take too many.
I whispered it hoping you wouldn't hear me
because I'm not ready

The signs are singing to my ears
and waving to my face
your opinions lies and truths
two of those screaming at my soul
then I gently whispered right back
They're invalid
Your plastic skin didn't like that

You knew I loved the moon and behind your back is a bag with a glow,
secret keeper: I often wonder why I couldn't feel the wind
I often wonder how many secrets the moon can take
If it were to explode I know we'd all die
the balance would be out of line
secrets would spill from the sky
which makes me think
you thought I was silly for talking to the moon
and now the moon is missing
you've hidden what I love but for what reason
did you try my therapy and feel dumb?
or do you want to hurt me?
I could believe both scenarios
It's been dark for weeks not just the sky but for us,
we were scheduled for a crescent today
but it didn't show so lets ask the moon about you.
let's hope it whispered to the clouds
so I can shower in your secrets
and you can shower in mine too

You took my hand instead of saying goodbye
thought you were down and angry losing interest in me,
thought you were leaving me the feelings you had for me,
my weakness is your sadness seeking my attention
every time I tell you what's running through my head
It's not supposed to make you pull away.
It's clearly a cry for help

Sad songs don't even
make me cry anymore

The way our planes take off in separate directions every time we meet up stings my heart. Why did we have to meet on a once in a lifetime trip. I can't help but count all fifty seven boarding passes every time I fly home after seeing you. Fifty eight now. Perhaps that brought us together because we're both stubborn when it comes to leaving our home.

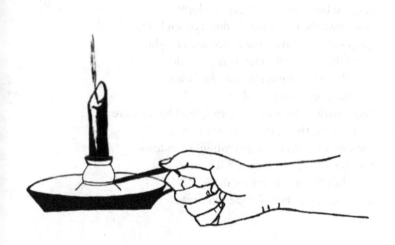

3:00 AM

Crescent Moon

The mask I hide behind remove it now.
look inside my eyes the window to my soul,
you know who I am when I don't even know,
I can't hide behind this shadow anymore,
I'll be waiting on that crescent moon,
to step across that dotted line and sit along that ledge so high,
remove the walls that block my light
stare into the midnight shadows down below
drop miles down on the reflection of light,
from that crescent moon sink deep down
into those midnight shadows far below
hit that ocean floor so slow.
those dark walls will wash away and be no more,
making me the light I'm meant to be,
the one who hid in those midnight shadows
will no longer be because I'll be me.
a midnight instrument for the muses
a shooting star here for the moments

Just like a memory card
music holds the memories
we made together

press play ▶

Dark ride

I know the pain that haunts your mind
I've been there before
we've been there before
we'll fight our way through this dark ride
sit side by side through the rough times
scream, cry and weep in each others arms.
After these times have passed
we'll both sit up so strong
stare straight out of our past
and enjoy this dark ride
link our hands together
say we're in this forever
then make it a lighter path
more than ever.

Let's not live in our horrible history
snowflakes or falling leaves
it is beautiful to see that
it is beautiful to let go
let us become something so sweet
something that won't rot our teeth

You're a diamond
I don't want to reshape
for my own personal satisfaction

Sugar Coat

Sprinkling sugar coats over my past,
stopping myself from remembering the bad,
is medicine to my mind. At least I think.
The poison are my friends and family that open my eyes
the feelings they throw at me when they say *remember when*
fill me with darkness from my feet and that dark liquid rises
making me tired and weak wanting to be free
taking off the coat is the strength I need
blowing off the sugar is what's meant to be
learning my friends and family are there for me
not the poison I thought they'd be
but they are strength for every inch of my being.
I am learning to cope and finding the paths to be free

Crying for someone to stay in your life
is like a child crying for candy.
If they stayed they would eventually rot your teeth.

Scars

There are scars on my arms and scars on my legs,
I walked through many storms went through many umbrellas
and even recycled the same old emotion just to keep going,
I approached every brick wall created every stepping stone and
hand hole,
Looking back at my past and looking mighty hard,
I thought I couldn't blossom with the lies and rumors
you spread throughout our town.
Weighing down on my shoulders is everything you said,
I placed a zip on your mouth so my ears couldn't hear,
continued with your talk to other ears mine couldn't hear,
I've walked through the feelings of failure,
climbed every prickly vine I rose up never better than anyone else,
just someone better than who I was before,
growing stronger and louder without your voice overpowering mine,
if I fall back I'll know my path after all
arrows that were shot were always pulled back

Our roots have spiraled out of control
linked up so tough our bond is unbreakable, I love you
like the waves swirl on and on for years at a time,
can we fix our broken halves or combine the perfect
half of our hearts to make a whole and live the love
we both dreamed to have together as one. Only us

Your beauty is unique,
It leaves me stunned my eyes so wide I want to move into that mind,
smiles sculpting eyes dimly close in awe at such a shining sight,
I love you
like the winds blow around the earth for decades at a time,
can we toss our broken halves in the trash and combine our perfect
half to make a whole and live the love we both dreamed to have
as one. Only us

Your beauty paints my smile and leaves me paralyzed,
like the stiffening of a used paintbrush
my eyes so wide they dimly close in awe
my mind wonders if I'm dreaming, I whisper no in reality.
I want to live in this sight
I want to live in this moment with you. I love you. Only us.

Put in some effort,
her heart will flutter with butterflies.

A good lesson from my Mother

I was a little boy alone at home with my mama. She bought me a cup of juice and as she was handing it over to me I spilled it all over the table. I was scared and I started to cry. She started wiping it up saying *it's okay my son, it's okay. These things can be cleaned up don't you worry* she began to hold me and tell me everything will be okay.

That taught me anger shouldn't be a go to emotion when something inconveniences you. You shouldn't put that fear in anyone but that you should be their peace. Be someone's comforting ear because accidents do happen and we can't really control it only learn from them.

Always be kind

now that I'm healed I'm kind of happy you broke my heart,
I was so broken and hurt before that I thought being with you
would heal me but being with you I broke even more,
then being without you I somehow found inner peace
and more bandages then I'll ever need

There is a line everyone has set
for their pain and you've crossed
mine now it's time to say goodbye

Watching people achieve what they have
always wanted to achieve has to be one of
the best feelings ever because after everything
they have been through and all the obstacles
they have endured and all the pain they took in.
They took a shot and did it

Message from the author
~

There are people always rooting for you.
Always believe in yourself and be proud
about how far you've come
I'm rooting for you

Growing again

Your broken promises hurt like the cracking of my ribs,
there is an echo in my empty heart from the excitement
that was disappointed.
The fossils of my organs began to soften and the first
thought in my mind was let's give this body one
more try at being alive.
My heart took a beat and I took a breath.
The zig zags on the machine were dancing of excitement

When the sun is covered
nature still moves forward
even without that little light
the birds still sing and take flight
the leaves still let go and
bring a beautiful sight
the snow still falls and shines bright.
always have strength in dark times
even if the pain is cold or hot.

Solitude is an enemy of mine that
I need to let in and make my best friend

Steps for when you are going through a rough time

Step one:

Pick a date from now to one week later. It can be longer if you'd like.

Step two:

Set an activity or a hobby to focus on for each day in between the dates you have picked. Whether it be a walk in the park, photography, writing, painting or creating and or starting something new.

Step three:

Stay focused on each day and promise yourself to fulfill your activities

Step four:

The feelings you had from what you were going through should start to heal by the release of emotions in the activity or hobby you have planned for yourself. Always check in with yourself and never forget that life is worth living for the little things. You always have the start of a healing journey

Message from the author
~
Keep chasing your dreams because there
is no one like you in this world.
You are your own unique and you deserve to live a
long happy life doing what you absolutely love.

Hezekiah Rory

How can you be the cure of my pain,
while you're the cause of it too.
How can you bring so much light
but have so much darkness
How can you bring so much comfort
but still have needles growing from your skin,
It doesn't make sense how I'm still in love with you
and even after everything
I still love you because I know I bring the same
storms to you and you still love me
after everything

Taking yourself back

I look inside the flicker of a flame until I'm sitting
inside like a time machine waiting and watching
everything go back to where our world was grey.
The flame was colored and I was let out to take the pain
for the poem I'm writing and release it in the form
of a beautiful truthful letter.
Taking myself back for the better
one letter at a time.

I need to know when you fall apart. I don't want to find a piece of you on the ground and wonder what happened. By the time I'll ask you'll be silenced by the thought of the cause of that frown. Someone who doesn't know your worth like you do deep down. I want to make sure I have every piece of you to help mould you back together when you can't do it by yourself. I want to be your artist for the broken feelings that are written on the bags under your eyes. I want to help cast your broken bones and heal the humor in your soul because a best friend stays forever

I begged at the feet of someone for them to stay
I cried and screamed, it felt so wrong.
After the cry and release of tears I felt dumb
and I was actually happy they were leaving.
My senses defended me and I let them

Beautiful, Free and Independent

When I bring you a flower I want it to be a reminder of how beautiful and strong you are. When it withers away I want you to remember why I picked it for you.

At a time you needed a guardian angel I picked you a guardian flower Yes, it withered but after the lifespan of that flower has gone you have come to believe and regain the love and self acceptance of how beautiful you are and you have been given strength to no longer need a guardian flower because you are a guardian flower. Time heals.

Heart Like You

How did I get a heart like you
Who takes me to the moon and safely brings me home
How did I get a heart like you
To hold me close and kiss my hand before you open the car door
How did I get a heart like you
Everyday you make a path of possibility for stuff I could never do
How did I get a heart like you
To hold me tight and squeeze my thighs
While we're watching a movie.
How did we get this way,
It's made a permanent grin upon my face
How did I get a heart like you
One who'd take his and replace it with my broken one

Your words cover me
and comfort me like a blanket
but your actions need to form a
layer over my heart. If you can't
provide that then we'll have to part.
I need more than words

You have a place in my mind
that's because I moved you out of my heart
and pretty soon you'll be out of my mind too

My mother peeked into my bedroom,
I saw the light against my wall with her dark silhouette
she saw the sheets of my bed in the shape of me,
I can only imagine how disappointed or worried she must be,
with her hand against the door and her sigh of... I don't know
but It couldn't have been a sigh of relief.
I see falling white threads creating sheets
which explains my clinomania
I hope it doesn't change into insomnia
I foresaw the wreckage my life will become if I continue
to lay in this bed,
I can't let that happen
I can't let you do this to me
though I'm heavy I'll be that empty skeleton in society.

For now

Sometimes you have to take
a trip down a path for the bits
and pieces that come with it
but you must return to your
road to use everything you
learned and survive

I have my own traumatic events that you can't make okay
If I tell you that I feel uncomfortable with something you
shouldn't try to find a way around it but it's your choice
I will not bring myself to control you

Create from your heart not your head,
for the head remembers others work
and the heart brings originality.
Bring your heart to life,
there is no other beauty than the beauty you hold inside.

Every morning your lips summon a kiss and
that's enough to bring me off the sheets

When you have the chance to do good. Do it.
Do not be blocked by the thought of deserve.
There was a time where you felt like you didn't
deserve anything and someone put that thought
away and covered you in kindness like a blanket

Stuck On Your Ex

There are times where your words sit in front of me
like being served bad dinner at a horrible diner.
My heart aches and my stomach clenches.
I cry when you tell me what you did with him by your
side while I'm shoveling a hole in the ground to bury
your words and memories you give me deep down they
go they aren't something I could carry. Oh, I wonder how
you can gently put these knives in my back.
I can't remove the memories from your head perhaps
if I was a witch I could cast a spell and distort your memories
like a bandage to a wound like Augustus Gloop to a
chocolate stream and Winnie the poo to honey jars you
were stuck on your ex and it wasn't fair to me
I pray our paths meet another time cause my sweet honey
I'm worth more than a treasure chest filled with sticky memories

All these *what ifs*
and we still met

Red Drop

I sit with the madness in your mouth,
I'm uncomfortable but just for you
to have you to hold you I'll stay,
itching through the weeks I'm secretly bleeding.
While I was cleaning I dropped a mirror
as I was picking up the pieces I saw different sides of myself,
my chin, my forehead, my eyes.
I stopped and stared at the pain I saw in my own eyes
then I dropped the glass because it pricked my finger
a red drop of blood landed on the broken pieces,
before I could get a tissue the drop slid on the
surface of every shattered piece.
I looked down and laughed,
my heart still flows with blood even when it shatters.

I know you have your daily battles
and your long term battles.
Just always remember that
you're still here and you're winning

Rhythmic Lines

I write these poems day and night
sobbing smiling or still in my fights
words flow into my brain in a rhythmic line
sometimes they fade in seconds
within this grasp of mine
failed attempts at writing them in time
lost letters, lost words
buried treasures of mine
you were a beautiful second in my head
till we meet again my rhythmic lines
I will get you and keep you safe in this journal of mine

He fell in love with me
so I can't let him change me
I'm saying that in a good way

Art is not meant to be perfect
It's about loving it the way you do
sloppy mistakes and all

Sadness is the doorway to my emotions
once I walk through I can do whatever I want
with whatever emotions I want because
I created them and others gifted them to me
whether it was road kill or diamonds
they're mine

The thing about heartbreak is that your ankles could be cut
two big stones could be on your shoulders
knives and arrows could be jabbed into your back
your organs could be dissolving
your bones could be noodles and
your bed could be summoning you,
even with all that pain life just
pushes you forward no matter how much you want time to stop.
Remember that you are strong enough.
You always have a reason to be strong enough.

Forgiveness is always open to you
but your apology will never bring
you back through the door

It's not too late to
run after me and grab my hand
It's not too late to
say you're there and that you'll stay
It's not too late to
say you're sorry
It's not too late

Remember the days when
the power would go out we would light
an old candle and never lanterns.
Every morning the candle would fade but
mama always had extra.
Pajamas and waterfall windows,
wood stove and family board games
hot tea and mamas homemade blankets
the comfort of childhood memories is
therapeutic to me

My mother has always
created an impossible path
just to help me in my times
of need

I Love You Mom

One day when we're old we'll look back together
in our home with a cup of tea in each of
our hands looking at each other from across
the room sitting on big comfy couches
and I'll say *I knew we'd make it through that*
then I'll walk over kiss you on the cheek
and say *I promised you I'd stay by your side*
then *boop* your nose

It was two different emotions
coming from the same set of eyes.
I'd see myself through yours and stare away
as fast as I can knowing what you're seeing.
I asked myself how can you love me and every time I did.
You'd tell me my heart was your favorite thing

I will pick at you
pinch you
pluck you
and carve you
just to get every piece of me back

You have that someone in your life
that is running through your head
right now because they always bring
a smile to your face and you know
you wouldn't have done it without them

Let's shoot arrows at the moon

I feel like the twinkle on the
star that comes once in a blue moon
but when I'm with you I feel like
the star while you're my moon

Insomnia

The day I hold the sun over my head
and it doesn't melt my hands
I'll no longer have darkness in my path
and tape over my mouth

Hezekiah Rory

Four After Midnight

Your pure beautiful smile drifts into my emotions
enough to cause a grin upon my frowning face.
Your eyes how they shine so bright lighting up my dark days
I can't see them in this moment but I
can feel you so close so warm
my head on your chest feels so much like a home I never had
peaceful, happy and comfortable.
The sound of your heartbeat is as calming as the waves
hitting the rocks on a quiet morning walk,
my mind can only think of reasons to stay awake
reasons to stay awake to spend more time
with such a handsome soul,
in these four walls in the dark four after midnight.
If I stared long enough I could see the darkness fade leaving
behind the silhouette of your beautiful face
a site that breathes life into my butterflies
there you are beside me
Four After Midnight

We are bound to die
and be put six feet under
when the time is right
we get shot up into the sky
like the earth is a bow and the
casket is an arrow

Surround yourself with happiness
even though it is found. It can be created.
Make unnecessary stress your enemy because
life is short and it offers happy little things,
mistakes are made and that's a good time to
remember you're living and learning.

Moments before I bumped into you my heart sank and my face blew up like my body knew. I thought I'd relive the hell you put me through but I just didn't care once I remembered you showed me who you were more times than necessary

The healing of a mother is something different.
I could have severe anxiety and the moment she places
her hands on mine she scares the darkness inside me away
like she has a light within her that flows into me.
Mothers are literally guardian angels.

I screamed at myself in the mirror
for being so dumb then I said *I love you*
to remind myself it's okay to make mistakes.
I did not shatter it.
I made peace with my reflection

If only a star was a rocket waiting for our souls
to reunite in the two seats of afterlife to become a light
upon this world for those who make a wish from
breathing land to a once dead star

Self Love

You make the flowers grow into a crown on my head
Your words flutter through the air like they were just purely born
into this world.
You bring color to everything around me and draw in the things
I'm missing
You sing like an angel when I'm feeling like the devil to change
the mood inside me
You bring happiness through a plate when I'm feeling down
You are me and I am happy

You could be giving and giving,
while everyone could be taking and taking,
know when your kindness is being
taken advantage of.
It's okay to say no

A fathers trust can
always teach you the
most greatest lessons

I feel as though I am running out of time and
running out of every sugar sweet dessert I've eaten
although I am broken writing is a bandage that slaps
itself on my wounds before I bleed out and fall into
the dark abyss. I will rise for the beautiful sunset
and not allow myself to dwell into the darkness
when I play with words I can write a ladder and
there is it sliding down into the cold scary hole
giving me a way out giving me the time I need to heal myself.
Writing is a gift and I intend to nurture it

Printed in the United States
By Bookmasters